I0541714

First paperback edition April 2024

Book design by Tobi Brun

ISBN 979-8-9902919-1-1 (Paperback)

Published by The Word's Faire
www.thewordsfaire.com

OF THE EATEN

Poetry and Prose

Tobi L. Brun

INDEX

FOR THE **CONSIDERATION** OF THE READER;

A: Does the modality of CONSUMPTION define the passing of TIME,

or;

the CONSUMPTION of seconds determine the TIME left to devour?

A: Once *face-to-face* with;

the beginning of
the end
of the beginning,

I MUST KNOW,
does the rebirth of death
taste sweetly or burn bitter?

EPIGRAPH

"We feed on babies, though not our own."
Robert Louis Stevenson

"Whenever I climb I am followed by a dog called 'Ego'."
Friedrich Nietzsche

"Children's meat was the best food of all in taste, followed by women and then men."
T'ao Tsung-yi

"We are, not aware, but awareness."
Mokokoma Mokhonoana

"How *sweetly* I do desire the end of the wheel."
A█████████

CANNIBALISM

(noun)

can·ni·bal·ism ˈka-nə-bə-ˌli-zəm

1: the ritualistic eating of human *flesh* by a human *being*.

2: the eating of the *flesh* of an animal by another animal of the same *kind*.

3: an act of cannibalizing something.

CHAPTER 5
THE INFANT

& Matters of the Body.

THE WHEEL

The Elder Eats The Adult.

The Adult Eats The Adolescent.

The Adolescent Eats The Youth.

The Youth Eats The Infant.

Fig. 01

The Living Room

The cherry-wood casket left pucker kisses on the carpet as
it was lifted away. It would only be picked and placed so
many more times, before its final release in the loam-cut
soil. Spiders hung and spun in the eaves, knitting lace as no
one remained to displace their work.
The remnants of the wake scattered among the evidence of
life, a dirt-shadowed footprint left scuffed onto once
meticulously kept furbishments, alongside half-sipped
flutes of Red.
Dust bunnies gather in multitudes of armed forces,
amassing troops underneath the out-of-date loungewear
that no one had sat on for a decade.

The removal of the casket displaced a tide of dust,
disturbing the air, the *still* air as *still* as an unfilled grave-
Human dust, the humans disturbed the human dust, full of
half-baked skin cells and sloughed off hair and

The grave of a room became the room that was the grave.
The grave of dust. The grave of dead dust.

[Sic]

The life is

[Sic]

The death is

[Sic]

Oxygen and LUNGS

Hungry and PAIN

More than i KNOW

AM I ALIV

[Sic]

Presence of being

SCREAMING

Held, am I held, I

[Sic]

Who am I?

I am, I?

Take I back in, IN IN IN

Not again, not again, not again

[Sic]

A... B... C...

A is for... ████████████████

B is for... bluhe, bluehbarees, boeyz.

C is for... *CAN YOU HEAR ME-*

D is for... dahgz, diyrt, drah.

E is for... *ESCAPE I NEED AN-*

G is for... gyrlz, goryllaz, gahs.

H is for... *HELP ME NOT AGAIN-*

I is for... eyeh, insiec, ise.

J is for... *JOKE COSMIC JOKE-*

K is for... kyss, kyndh, kyd.

L is for... *LOST THE BET*

M is for... mahm, milk, mahl.

N is for... *NOTHING COULD BE WORSE-*

O is for... opin, o clowk, owl.

P is for... *PLEASE, HAVE MERCY-*

Q is for... quilt, quik, quiet.

R is for... *rescue me from this wheel-*

S is for... soft, sofa, silence.

T is for... *this life will be different-*

U is for... ugly, umbrella,

V is for... *vast hunger will consume*

W is for... win,

X is for...
Y is for...
Z is for...

A LIST OF THOUGHTS IMPORTANT TO A SEVEN-YEAR-OLD.

1. she pushed my block tower down! i HATE her!
2. mommy and daddy yell too loud.
3. daddy is MEAN.
4. mommy is MEAN.
5. i dont like the yogurt chunks in my cereal.
6. sometimes i dream of drowning until i remember i can breathe.
7. my friends laugh sometimes when i'm not there, but i can hear, and it makes me sad.
8. horses are SO cute.
9. sometimes i dream of a building far away, with a tall shadow that watches me from the door.
10. i HATE wearing socks, they crunch around my ankles, itchy!
11. mommy hurts my head when she brushes my hair.
12. sometimes i dream of my street and my grandparent's house, completely empty, no people anywhere.
13. i wonder who i will be when my age is times two.
14. sometimes i dream of █████████████████████

THE ASPHODEL MEADOWS

There is a baby (A Child!)
in the Asphodel fields.
The child is touching (Eating!)
the tender white buds.
What should we do (Cursed!)
to stop it?
Its fingers bend (Flesh!)
so delicate and supple.

It dreams.
It speaks.
What does it say?
Lean in close.

"█████████████"

I know you, (Run!)
I know your voice.
I met you once in a previous life.
How the mighty have fallen,
or perhaps, have forgotten.

Careful child,
your fingers will stain too red from that blood.

???

You ███████ can ████████ feel ████ me? ███████ I ████████ know ██ you're ███████ there. Don't ████ be ███ scared. I ██ am ████ sorry. ███ The ████ Wheel ████ must ████ end. ████ Don't ███ you ███ mind ███ the ████ pain. ███

A Collection

1. *A Rock Collection*
   a. Mica, Quartz, Geodes, Sandstone, Shale, Jasper, Agate, Flint, Gypsum.

   > The pads of fingers
   > run over the
   > edges.
   > Oh!
   > good rock.
   > good rock.
   > good rock.

2. *A Memory Collection*
   a. A corner of memorabilia. Broken skateboard, cracked in the middle. Cabbage patch doll, tattered and frail. Books with ghosts trapped between the pages. Sketchbook of bodies, eyes, and boy girls. Too many yearbooks, spines cracked.

3. *The Collection of Movement*
   a. Boxes of boxes; the rediscovery of possessions with the adrenaline release

of lost treasure unearthed amongst the rubble.

4. *A Collection of Achievements*
   a. First grade sits high on a shelf, second grade under coats in the closet. Third grade hides underneath a box full of child-size shoes. The best of the best rests in a pile on top of the fridge retired from its prime real estate.

5. *A Collection of* ████████████████
   a. Sweetling, tastes of handfuls of blueberries, and bitter notes of bark scraped knees on the schoolyard playground.
      Tears tasting each sea salt sweetness, lick my wounds and pick up the pieces.
      Inner voices speak in mumbles, lap them up. They sit like stones in a stomach that doesn't exist.

Power

The first time power was stolen,
Pin-pricked smile sewn into supple skin.

The second time power was stolen,
Shoes eating anxious feet, and dancing toes.

The third time power was stolen,
Hairbrush bristles caught bloody; itching scalps.

Power was stolen,

Power is stolen,

Power taken.

CHAPTER 4
THE YOUTH

& Matters of the Mind.

Fig. 02

The Master Bedroom

The ceiling is puckered, dappled with stucco fireworks.
Twin laser-eyed holes simmer; hours of staring into the
dissociated darkness.
Piles shape shadows, thin laundry hampers make shadow
puppets;
body dysmorphia heaped onto depressive episodes.
Mirror hanging over the mantle piece; hinting at ghosted
imprints of bodies, shifting squeezing shaping. Sexuality
arching, fogging up the silver-tinted glass.
The closet door bulges around the edges, holding back the
tides of steaming hot piles of ripe depression-soaked
laundry.
Under the bed, shoved and wrinkled.
It hides there.
one-night-stands and social gatherings.
11:11pm s and 'I'll never be enough' s.
abandoned amazon boxed hobbies and knobbly bruised
knees.
The covers are made lightly, crisp with hospital-folded
corners. Pillows freshly plumped, regardless of headless
dents.

On the Line

A decade, ten years, 3650 days.
Momentous feelings of newfound adequacy taste of
ice cream cookie cake melted onto Disney paper
plates.
Ten feels like no other age,

Trust me I know.
It never feels the same, maybe sixty, a hundred feels
close,
Feelings taste of stale air later in life a long.

Nevermind.
Never *you* mind.

Nothing is not nice now, for now,
new eyes, so fresh, so fleeting,
full of so so so

Ten feels like no other age.

Puberty

Age is hungry
Feasting on the insides of black heart boy girl

Watch it eat
A fascinating thing
Ritualized consumption of
Bleeding and Eating

Has been known to cause side effects...
Nausea

Vomiting

Diarrhea

Aging

Eating

Licking

Crying

Growing

Moping

Needing

And eventual... Death.

A Dream Within A Dream

"Why am I…"

"Like this?"

"Yes, this. This…"

"This mind. This body."

"Yes. All of that."

"It was chosen for you."

"By who?"

"By… ██████████"

"I don't…"

"Understand?"

"…"

"You may never understand."

"The wheel…"

"Will turn."

"Forever."

The Menu

Question: What does it taste like when a heart breaks?
Answer: It tastes like...

It tastes like hot-cold messy bodied scribbles, skin scratching, bitten bloody tongues.

Question: What does it taste like when friendships expire?
Answer: It tastes like...

It tastes like curdled, boxed-up memories. Sour and saccharine, scintillating suspicion.

Question: What does it taste like when innocence is lost?
Answer: It tastes like...

It tastes like pretentious poetry. It claims to have the meaning, the answers. Like answers sleeping sweetly between the lines.

Magic

Look into an animal's eyes.
Blink once for yes,
Blink twice for no.

"Do you understand me?"

Childhood dies,
In the palm of
an involuntary realization.

Delicious

Humph and hah.
Building back better, and better
And better!
Build upon backbones
Break down bodies

Want to know a secret?
Inside the flesh,
Deep inside my burrows of marrow,
That's me.
I'm you, you're me.

Caged in glass, in glass-cased bones.
It drips, endlessly.
Coated, sloppy, drenched.

Blood, marrow, plasma, tears, bile, and burning acid.
Sucking fingers, lapping up the spills,
You keep me busy.

I'm never alone, you haunt me.
Ghosted flavors of humanity;
contaminated filthy tastes.
Being alive tastes like dead birds, I think.
Dead *dead* birds buried under loam,
Soaking and boiling in the crimes of the earth

Bodies breaking under diamond pressure.

Humans taste like blood, I know.
Boiling bodily blood.
It's sweet on the tongue,
But cold in the stomach.

All I could ever know is

Blessed Bones

Rattling these blessed bones,
Headache-bleeding-eyeball-migraines!

Falling in love for the first time (or Last?)

It glows neon ember signage along the highways,

Never look back again,
Never leave the trail ahead (Behind?)

Tangled up inside of blessed bones,
Sticky feels-like-love
stuck inside. All balled up and brave.

Fall in love,
Again and again and again and again and
Discovery of touch on touch, *electric.*

It tastes like rain. Like stuck-in-the-rain.
Like stuck-in-the-rain-under-the-same-umbrella.

Pleading and Pondering.
It's a virus,
It cuts, and burns.

It infects the bones, cutting deep with blades of flower petals.

Sticky sap of
What's-meant-to-be-will-be
And
Right-person-wrong-time

Drips and drowns
Sizzles where it lands.

I knew of love once.
Many, many times over.

CHAPTER 3
THE ADOLESCENT

& Matters of the Spirit.

Fig. 03

The Kitchen

Kitchen is home base, ground zero, headquarters,
stomping grounds, hospital, hoarding zone,

                Standing room.
"I'm *disappointed* in you-"
"Back in *my* day-"
"Come *right* back here and finish-"
"Your mother and I have been *talking*-"
"We don't think you should see *them* anymore-"

Yellow walls. Growing up in a kitchen with yellow walls.
All kitchens should have yellow walls.

A teenager in a kitchen is a moth after the light switch flips.

A teenager in a kitchen is future bound, yellow walls,
produce ripe, happy food, with breathing room.

A teenager stuck in a kitchen is an adult who avoids one.

Well, Well, Well.

An argument of existence is Caught between two places.

Dependency and Questions.
Answers and Independence.

Do the math!
Look over your shoulder!
Always ahead!
Never back, never behind!
Well,

Formulaic years, charted and graphed ahead.
Steps and stairs and
Who's that pushing from behind?
It's ████████

The answer is solved, show your work.
Well,
The wheel turns.

(The answer exists at the beginning of the equation.)
Well.

Ribcage

Feel ribs fit to burst,
Breathe deep oxygen, commanding space.
Watch in rapt attent.

EXPANSION
CONTRACTION

In and Out and In and Out and
It works itself-
machine man-made.

No life is lost in between the space.
Fascinating.

The realization of each mechanism;
Anxiety bites back, iron age drums beating.

FIGHT OR FLIGHT
Right?
Off to war...
Off to score,
Fit to burst. Fit to burst.

Deep-Fried Renaissance

Kissing boys and kissing girls.
Sucking souls,

       Drink them all down,
        Yes, that's it.

Soul fire caught in the throat,
Burning bright-white nights,
Bubbling lovely scars,

         All the way,
          Down.

     Tasted sour.
     Tasted honey.
     Tasted human.
     Tasted burnt.

         Take it **back**,
         No **more**,

Too late!
Lips locked in,
Puzzle-pieced-up souls,
Tumbledown.

    Human Spit and Bitten lips.
   Nevermore sick, just missing the best bits.

Fetish

Stuck in spaces between dreams;
Squeezing tight between the thick bricked walls,
Something is moving?
Something is, beating.
Something is twisting
Building, Changing, writhing,

Transformation!

Blood is moving.
Skin is shaping.

Stuck.
Too Big.
Stuck.

Who are you?

Who are you now?

Who will you be?

Proposition.

Form the line,

                  Pick your poison!

Must decide,

                  Or risk a deny!

Take a bite,

                  Chew and swallow!

No fate,

                  Never too late!

Pass or fail,

                  Learn the lesson!

Navigate,

                  Stop and Wait!

Alone,

                  Look and See!

You will,

                  Last!

Live,

                  Longer!

...

The edge...

It's deep.

What's below?

The other side,

Burning bridges.

Making marks.

Adulthood recognizes me.

Cast blame in you.

White flag,

Can't lie,

After it's all done,

We're just the same,
The villain.

Beckoning us,

Beyond the sea.

Can you see?

Or am I,

Alone.

A is for...

Your obsession with humanity began in God's backyard.
You were watching humanity from the place that you can
always see, but your eyes slide right over, past the eyes
staring back at you that you're not quite ready to meet yet.
You couldn't understand the way the humans
birthed and ate and drank and fought and killed and
fucked and died,
sometimes for each other.
Silly little playthings running amok
on It's-perfect-world.
We all knew the end, what was going to happen at the end
of Its little experiment.
That was known well before the beginning,
of It that is.
God desired death.
God created humanity.
Humans would kill God,
First,
they had to learn its secrets.
It was taking ages back then, far too long before things
were going to get interesting.
You, decided to make things interesting.
You decided to... play around. Muddle things up.
You created a disease,
a sickness, an infection.
It wormed inside their brains;

scooped out their rational thoughts to create one-track
obsessions.
Some part of you thought this might speed along the
process.
It worked!
They began to succumb at lightning speed, the disease
spreading across the tiny planet.
It spawned a wave of civilizations, wars, fanatics,
massacres, renaissances. The issue only began, when we
began to fall sick.
You had loved interfering with the human's world,
one day You got too close.
You saw things You had *never* seen before from far away,
the distance brought everything into focus.
You brought the disease back with you.
It ate out your thoughts,
you, you fell in *love*.
You fell in love with *Her*.
God's wife.
Asherah.
You worshiped her,
You craved her,
You ate her up.
You began to *desire*,
something we were never meant to do.
It broke down your essence, and you became something
other.
Something far too human

for being unhuman.

You *loved* Her,

what could you do but keep loving Her?

She was the face of each human that fell in love.

It knew,

It watched; but did nothing.

It watched you fall, did nothing.

It knew the cost, did nothing.

After crime, comes the punishment.

You wanted to be human, You wanted to love?

Your punishment, become each human,

Devour each human from the inside out.

As you tainted their purposeless lives with your purposeful disease.

You became the consequence of your desire.

You became *it*.

You became you.

You became *God*.

You were gone,

You thought you would never think again.

Yet here, you remain.

Stuck between the lines,

Caught between the DNA.

It's *different*.

Why?

Tell us God, *why?*

CHAPTER 2
THE ADULT

& Matters of the Heart.

Fig. 04

The Backyard

Time to get lost. Time to lock the door on the way out and sit in the dirt, and sink each fingertip deeper until the soil wets skin. Playing make-believe, passing time, passing ages, passing centuries.
Adventure, intrigue, mystery, murder, caught up in the thrill-of-it-all. Lock the windows, stay outside.

Forehead kisses, and gardening gloves,
Poisonous flowers, and Miracle moss.
Buried treasure, and hand drawn maps.

The end of summer is cooking on the pavement,
Pushpop popsicle sticks left discarded in puddles of sugar.

Telling stories on the first stage, disturbed dust settles loose on ground yearning to be stepped, kicked, danced on and thrown.

It's waiting out there, it's still waiting.

Bubblegum

Rest assured, they know it when they've lost it.
It leaves an imprint, a scar, a gap in the flesh.
It tears away in cords and bundles,
Poking needles and pinched cheeks.

They taste the afterglow on their tongues and lick the last
remaining drops of bloodied memories from their skin.

They know it when they've lost it-
because they'll never know it again.

They need and crave it too much,
Clawing round their interspaced memorial grounds,
Rasping, pleading, and dying.

They know it when they've lost it,

Because it's the beginning of the end.

Now, What?

It's Six AM.

Stretching...
Breathing...
Still Alive.

Feeling old at Six AM.
Muscles feel thin, at Six AM.
Airtight and cold, at Six AM.

Toes stubbed on corners, at Six AM.
Fingers burned on full coffee cups, at Six AM.
Feeling like crying, at Six AM.

Watching the sunrise at Seven AM.

Adult is Six AM.

Highway

Drive-by,
Hang on,
Not too fast,
Windows cracked,
Dial maxed,
White little lines,
Traffic-stop,
Just in time.

Wind fingers,
Minute timers,
Open cup holders,
Ghost sirens.

Back road,
By-way,
Litter bug,
"My Way".

Taxes

Pay to live!

Pay to drink!

Pay to procreate!

Pay to smile!

Pay to hide!

Pay to play!

Pay to mind!

Pay to go!

Pay to lie!

Pay to grow!

Pay to improve!

Pay to die!

Rejection

Raised eyebrows; outside the circle.
Jail Time in Monopoly.
Canceled plans, last minute.
Regular days; the boring ones.

Notices in the mail.
Emails; the misleading kind.
The day after a birthday.

College decisions.
Childhood heroes; the tainted admiration.
Recognizing manipulation.

Sticky.
Sorry.
Bye.

Grocery-Shopping

1. Produce

Carrots for the eyes.
Spinach for the heart.
Garlic to heal sickness.

It's not enough.

2. Dairy

Cheese for the calcium.
Milk for the protein.
Yogurt for the probiotic.

It's not enough.

3. Pantry

Peanut butter for the magnesium.
Honey for the antioxidants.
Oils for the minerals.

It's not enough.

Mid-Life.

"Quiet now."

                          "Wasn't the youth of it enough?"

"Too quiet now."

                          "Hm, ate it all?"

"Not at fault."

                          "Yes, it is."

"Not forever."

                          "Not again."

"Break the wheel."

                          "Not enough time."

                It's never enough time.

Sex Coded

Yes. No.
Drink it. Choking.
Raging. Crying.
BROKEN. Mending.
Nature's coding. Foreign bodies.
Lick it. Kiss it.
Losing. Winning.
Heaven-bound. Underground.
Scream louder. Whisper more.
Dying. Living.

Explore,
Tell me more,
Fell behind,
Crossed each line.

Preserve me, ███████

CHAPTER 1
THE ELDER

& Matters of Time.

Fig. 05

The Nursery.

The Drinking, The Eating, The Gasping, The Seeing, The Touching.

The light is too bright, too warm, too cold. Squint, but no eyelashes to catch the sun. The air is too large in the lungs, to wail on, to scream on, to laugh on.

The throat is greedy, the stomach is too small. The limbs must grow, make room. Now, faster, quicker, bigger.

The bottom of the world is beneath, the sky is above, and the faces that hover are known and wanted.

It all checks out, just right. New beginnings. But the end remains. The end of safety in the womb, the end of the body as it breathes in oxygen. The end of eternity as mortality is thrust inside.

The beginning of the end
is always at
the beginning.

Sunset Season

Taste goes first.

Wrapped around the ring finger.

Caught in the hair stuck in the drain.

Kissed onto sun spots and varicose veins.

Shaking in the *Live-Forever* box.

Slipping in the shower.

Stuck in the blank spaces.

Missing at the holidays.

Wishing for the pain to stop.

Looking for the old hangs.

Contemplating in the closet.

Negotiating at the doctor's office.

Crying at friends' funerals.

Skimming through the paperwork.

Sitting in the sun.

Learning relaxation.

Navigating mixed emotions.

Bland.

Legacy

Philosophical moods catch cold in the twilight.
Come inside, get a coat.
Watch the sky, and become into starlight.
The moon likes the sight of Earth.

Regret.

Regret.

Should've listened to *FILL IN THE BLANK*.
Why didn't I *FILL IN THE BLANK*.
Never thought it would *FILL IN THE BLANK*.

Come inside.
It's cold.

The moon looks away sometimes,
Can't stand the sight.

Kiss the cold, and recognize the taste.
Is that,
It couldn't be,

SPIT IT OUT.

IV - High

RX: FOUNTAIN OF YOUTH

PATIENT NAME: A█████████████

ADDRESS: Beneath the BONES of it ALL

PRESCRIPTION:

Enjoy what's left. Breathe the oxygen, that's left. Drink and Eat, that's left. Bask and Reap in, that's left.

Stop looking back, look up. Look down. Look what is held too tight in broken finger bones.

Existence is reduced to the pigeon holes deep in gray matter.

Put in a thumb, and pull out a plum.

What a good boy am I!

REFILLS: 999,999 REMAINING
Exp. Infinite Beginnings

Signature: Humanity

Computations

Thought without thought is what = /null

Brain without voice is what = /empty

Child without parent is what = /childless

Life without Death is what = /theWheel

God without hell is what = /theDevil

Ancestry without a story is what = /bygone

A body without muscle is what = /marionette

Flesh inside of flesh is what = /aPromise

A face in the mirror is what = /slipping

Love without body is what = /buried

Sight without seeing is what = /aGhost

Message without a sender is what = /DNA

A is...

Biggest burrowing brain boughs.

Catharsis catching cutthroat closing.

Drowning dire degrees.

Escaping enunciated entire eras.

Feelings fire faster, further.

Gather growing garbage.

Hitting highs hoping hallows.

Incredibly insincere.

Justifying jokes.

Killing.

Left.

Movement.

Negotiating never none.

Overture-only opening.

Possibilities posing peace.

Quiet.

Rising resistance.

Saving salutations salvaging sanctity.

Trusting tribulations.

Under ugly unity.

Variety vaccinates vows.

Wonder.

Xenic.

Zenith.

Simplistic

Sunrises are golden coins, spent in a coin toss-
  Anotha' day anotha' dollah.
 Morning cups of coffee tasting of dirt and home.
  To be held, to be thought of.
Cupboards of birthday cards- used and unused.
  Bright lights, loud sounds, hot food.
Pill boxes rattle-
  Gravity sits on broken shoulders.
Flowers sprouting, crack through blistered finger webs.

  Lungs burn bright blood vessels;
  A Locomotive Engine.

  Mouth full of dirt,
  Stomach lined with lead.
  Feet grow long and toes unscrew...

Ready is a concept, happy is just a word.
  Embroider each fingertip with the names,
  The ones not to be forgotten.

Facing East

"Dogs face East to die."

                                        "Why?"

"Dolphins have funerals for their dead."

                                        "Why?"

"Monkeys mummify their dead."

                                        "Why?"

"Elephants bury their dead."

                                        "Why?"

"Crows have vigils for their dying."

                                        "Why?"

"You're dying."

                                        "Why?"

Of The Eaten

death in the blink of an eye
a rasp between the lips
Tumbling and caving in all around
blood in the feet
Again.

"What becomes of the eaten?"

"Have you learned?"

BREATHE IN
BREATHE O

FOR THE **DISCRETION** OF THE READER;

A: I know you well, dear one. I am you.

A: We met many times, many lives.

M: Humanity is my disease,

O: and my greatest pride.

N: Live, and be well.

ACKNOWLEDGMENTS

To those where credit is due;

Thank you first to the readers. In your hands, you hold a copy of my first published work, from my indie publishing company *The Word's Faire*. Having acquired this copy, this means you have supported my business and creative community. Thank you deeply for supporting the creative side of life.

Thank you to my family, my grandparents, and my friends, mentors, and teachers throughout my life so far. The support, beta reading, and love you have gifted me have molded me into the person I am today. Thank you to my Grandmom for always being my first reader. Thank you to my middle school teachers, Mr. Madigan and Mrs. Henry who taught me not to lose my creative side. Thank you to my college professors, and especially to Dr. Erin Flanagan who has been a constant supporter and recommendation-writer.

Thank you to Taylor Kingston who has mentored me in my educator role, and to all of my students who have reminded me of the childhood love of creative things.

Thank you to Noah, Beth, Percy, Kol, Emily, and Christine.

Final thanks to Ghostlight Coffee for creating a space for me to write this collection in the dead of winter 2022.

ABOUT THE AUTHOR

Tobi Brun is chronically obsessed with the human condition, loves their cats, and is probably up past their bedtime. Tobi is a creative writing adjunct, barista, and a burnt-out 20-something looking for the meaning of life. They write fiction, poetry, and prose. Tobi is a Dayton native writer, educator, and founder of the Indie Publishing Press 'The Word's Faire'. Tobi is a Wright State grad with a BA in English and writes experimental short fiction and prose. They enjoy listening to horror podcasts while sipping a strong cup of tea and cuddling their two cats Ronny and Ravi. One could find them lying in the sun, or peeking around corners.

Find More from Tobi at *thewordsfaire.com*

www.ingramcontent.com/pod-product-compliance
Lightning Source LLC
Chambersburg PA
CBHW051554120626
46551CB00013B/1507